Babi Yar
and other poems

Herbert Druker

Wordrunner Press

Babi Yar and other poems

© 2020 by Herbert Druker

ISBN: 978-1-941066-40-9

Wordrunner Press
Petaluma, California

Contents

Babi Yar	1
Tears	2
Two Prose Poems From My Youth	3
At the Cemetery	4
Inner Vision	5
Expectations	6
The Bus Stop	7
Mental Sinkhole	8
Painting	9
On Having a Painting Critiqued	10
Unresolved	11
Conversation	12
The Shirt	13
The Chair	14
Coats	15
How Will You Mourn for Me	16
At Peace	17
Nap	18
Later Years	19
Leaves	20
Fireworks	21
Halloween	22
Valentine	23
Loss – 1	24
A Day	25
Fate	28
Missing	31
Loss – 2	32
Last Things	33
Losing You	34

Today	35
Death, Expected	36
Lost Memories	37
Identity	38
Once Again	39
Bliss	40
The Rainbow	41
Forsythia	42
On the Bay	43
Inner Visions	44
Small Enjoyments	45
The Good Life	46
Alone	47
Autumn	48
Fishing	49
The Lake	50
Togetherness	51
Larry	52
Steve	53
Doris	54
Election Day	55
Touching	56
Perspective	57
Beginning	58

Babi Yar
and Other Poems

Babi Yar

I have walked by the covered banks of Babi Yar
It is a tranquil place
Like Lidice
Beyond this generation there will be history books
Or perhaps a bronze plaque
Commemorating…..

I have been under the trees near Babi Yar
The shade is pleasant
Images collect in the periphery of my consciousness
Of butchery at Belsen
Atrocities at Auschwitz

I have watched the birds cavort above Babi Yar
They know it only as a feeding place
Like the beaches at Dunkirk
Or the phoenix city of Stalingrad
Time has transformed the ugliness

I have listened to the silence at Babi Yar
The echoes of leaders' voices ring clearly
Little changed from today's strident tones
Hurrying humans into hysteria
And destruction of each other

The ground is fertile at Babi Yar

Tears

The tears come unbidden
from a place within me
I ache to know but have been unable to find.
It repeatedly eludes me.

Are the tears an homage to my father
whose family I could never meet?
A remembrance of his pain and loss
catapulted into the present?

Are they recognition of my own mortality
as I confront the horror of the destruction
of people I never knew?
I wipe my face and eyes.

Two Prose Poems From My Youth

The house became quieter and quieter until even normal conversation was an intrusion on the sorrowful stillness shrouding every room. The door to his bedroom opened when an adult entered and if I stood nearby I could hear the hollow hacking that conjured tortured visions before I fell asleep at night. I gave a silent sigh when my mother tearfully announced that he had "passed away" during the night. It was my first meeting with death.

I never forgave my mother for so incensing my father that for the first time in his life he hit me across the face hard enough to leave red welts not cooled by tears that ran endlessly despite my effort to stop them and regain control of myself. She berated him for hitting me on the face but he was in such turmoil he strode away letting her words fall harmlessly on his back.

At the Cemetery

My eyes examine the hole in the ground
Watching the brown box slowly descending
Almost catching on the sides
As it moves to its resting place.

The image of you appears within my eyes,
Taller than me, more solid,
Thinning hair, small lips and a lumpy face.
What captures me is the essence that is you
Beyond the physical,
The personality that meshes with me.

I try to hold on to you,
To keep you with me,
Unable to confront my loss.
Voices blur since I refuse to hear.

At the end of the ritual
I take up one of the shovels, dig fully into the piled up dirt,
Putting my share of earth
On the already partially covered coffin.
Only then do I feel cold,
Only then can I say farewell.

Inner Vision

The breeze slides across the leaves
Creating soft rustlings
That enter my open bedroom window
I listen to its delicacy
Diligently trying to recreate
The picture of its creation

Expectations

Have you noticed
That sometimes
Things for which you have low expectations
Surprise, and give unexpected pleasure,
Delighting beyond the mere event?

Of course you need to be willing to allow them in,
Putting aside mind frozen attitudes
That would not let the experience bubble to the surface.

The Bus Stop

People standing, sitting patiently
Pacing or just leaning on a wall as if asleep.
Waiting, waiting, waiting, waiting, waiting
Is the focus on the small, surrounding world of the bus stop?
Are there thoughts active in the mind?
Or does it go blank
With the knowledge that time continues to move forward?

To wait on a rare occasion or even once in a while
Makes it a novelty
But daily
As a necessity to reach a job
To visit a relative or friend
Creates a high, wailing, smoldering scream
At the unfairness of life
Until throttled in order to survive
A nagging reminder of underclass position
With little hope of ever enjoying the luxuries
Others take for granted.

Mental Sinkhole

What kind of mental sinkhole
Contains the pieces that attract and repulse
Almost unknowingly until the stirring
Becomes a conscious sensation that is recognized.

Today the balm of music surrounds me
Filling me with satisfaction as I see the contentment on your face.
As you respond to the sound it reinforces our kinship
Adding to the mesh that binds us together.

The voice drones on and on
Until I mentally go away
Not caring if the message is worth hearing.
The grating closes me to the message.
The message closes me to the mind
That creates it.
I walk away.

Painting

The model sits in front of me
Draped carefully in the chair,
Staring vacant eyed,
With an occasional small tremor
To prove she is still alive.

I wonder where her thoughts have wandered
Does she need to concentrate on her body
To hold the pose or
Does a coming evening's entertainment
Occupy her as she sits?

I force myself to look at her,
Decide on color and shape,
Painting begins.

On Having a Painting Critiqued

I was crushed by you tonight
You didn't mean to do that
But I know you
The positive comments as you reviewed many of the others
balanced by suggestions for improvement
reinforced my admiration for your teaching technique.
Until you came to me
"Play more," you said. "Enjoy the paint," you said
"Be bolder, be freer."
I felt my body get hot
My eyes lost their focus
I wanted to run away but could not
So, as you moved down the line
I prepared to flee
Was there nothing worthwhile in my effort?
I must try again

Unresolved

I ask myself
Can you take a failed painting
And turn it into a success by collage? If the elements don't work together,
The forms attempted do not convey their meaning,
Wouldn't the result best be placed at the bottom of some pile
Or perhaps be done away with altogether.

I keep it because I can not confront the failure.
I hope to rescue it,
To overlay some connection
That will enable me to feel the success
I thought was going to appear when I began.

Conversation

She was vivacious, attractive and intelligent
As I participated in the group's conversation
Our eyes met and glanced away

Did I read too much in the soft smile?
I waited
As I spoke her eyes seemed to caress me

A surge of sudden warmth suffused my face
Indecisive
I could only lock my eyes on her

Waiting for another brief contact
That sent irrational thoughts cascading
Until I realized the conversation had moved on

Dinner was ending
Desperately I moved towards her
To see whether there was more than her glance available

The Shirt

Here is the shirt
You left one night
I ache
From thoughts of acrobatics
My flesh can no longer handle
Even in memory

The shirt hangs unworn
A testimony
To shimmering nights
In other cities
That excited our entwined hands
And later our entangled bodies

The Chair

Last week while on the interstate
I passed a chair lying on its side just off the edge of the highway
The brown leather looked better than many I've seen
Could it have fallen out of a vehicle and not been noticed?
Deliberately dumped?
Was there a flaw not visible from an automobile traveling at
 highway speed?
Could someone fix it and use it?
Was it an example of how we view the world
Or how we treat each other?

Coats

I watched him leaving the hospital
with a woman's coat over his arm.
Clearly,
she would not need it.
The sunglasses he wore
could not conceal his wet face,
nor his bafflement.
As if in mockery
the day was fair and the air
mild for November.
Despite the sun's warmth he had zipped his coat,
tied the hood under his chin,
prepared for the cold.

How Will You Mourn for Me

How will you mourn for me
When my body lies covered o'er
Meditate neath a tree
Watch waves wash the shore

How soon will time dull the memory
Of the friendship we now hold so dear
How much will time our emery
Grind away from thought each year

At Peace

I notice my eyes
fill up more often than ever before.
Are my hormones out of balance?
Is it age?

I am free of the restraints needed
while aspiring towards career goals.
I can now permit experience to flow over me,
allowing myself to feel in ways
I would not consider before.

I have come to appreciate
the wonders of the world around me.
Tears are the measure of my contentment.

Nap

I tried to take a nap this afternoon
Lying there, eyes closed, without sleeping

However, it marked a milestone
Admitting that my body needed rest during the day

An acknowledgement that age
Had finally caught up to me

I hated that recognition but succumbed to it
For so long naps were for the energy depleted

And I, reluctantly, crying inside my head, had joined them
People that nap have greater longevity I've been told

I wonder whether all the additional life is the time lost taking naps

Later Years

I have dutifully read
The authorities
Telling me in Serious tones
How important it is to live life
In ways that will improve and extend it
As a younger person I tried very hard
To follow their advice
Often succeeding

Now in my later years
I question
Neither their wisdom nor their correctness
But the shortsightedness of following
Their advice forever
How many pleasures have I denied myself
For an increase in existence

As a younger person
Looking at older people behaving disastrously
I failed to understand the concept
"Enjoy it now the end is in sight."
It was lost upon me
Until I became old enough to be like them myself

Leaves

The leaf rocks back and forth
Slowly making widening circles
As it falls gently to the Earth

I lose it in the mass that is on the ground
Matted from the rain of last evening
No longer attractive and individualized

Another leaf catches my eye
As it swirls and swoops
Until it too touches the ground

How often do most humans
Flutter away at the end
To become indistinguishable

Fireworks

Earlier this evening I watched a fireworks display
It reminded me of times past
When each thunderclap of sound and burst of color
Elicited oohs and ahs of pleasure
And held populations transfixed
Necks arched, eyes eagerly searching for the next explosion in the sky above

Accounts in newspapers early in the last century
Drip with excitement
Glow with the newness of the experience
Comparing the latest display to those before it

For me
The fireworks presented almost nothing new,
Nothing spectacular
How often does the excitement of one time
Become the ignored commonplace of the next

Halloween

Trick or treating was an aggravation for me. It was a ritual to be endured in order to get to November. My costume, put on reluctantly, made me feel weird. Sweeping me along with them, my friends were excited, chatty, and full of nonsense. I felt distant from them, annoyed since there was no enjoyment for me. I thought, "There are no more witches, goblins, and ghosts." Trick or treating had become a pale sham for collecting candy, apples, and bits and pieces of gum. I regret not having had the courage to say, "I don't want to go."

Valentine

Please accept my heart once more
Even though it doesn't matter
For served up dripping on a platter
Full of blood and dangling tubes galore
There is little to commend it

Yet within its proper cavern
It squirts and squirms in certain ways
When you are about me, that the days
Of absence from you are wan and thin
In a vital warm dimension

Have it either way you choose
Its thumping is for today all yours
Wrapped in body or in gauze
Though personally I do enthuse
A preference for the former

Loss – 1

When I moved to this oasis far from town
the nearest neighbor was a comfortable mile away.
My trees rustled contentedly
providing a soft musical program
that wrapped me in cloistered serenity.
It took me a while to recognize their conversation.

The green barrier that I enjoy diminishes.
It no longer keeps sounds and voices
from intruding into my space.
The music has almost lost its melody.
Angry tones disturb my sleep
as they moan the loss of friends now gone forever.

A Day

I put my hands on the little engraved silver cup
Found in the overgrown meadow
Not realizing the power it had for me
Crystal zigzag lines ran across my vision
A surge of hidden experience overwhelmed me
As I recovered I bent and picked up the cup
Holding it gingerly, arm extended
As if keeping it close would shock me again
Cause the vision and the experience to imprint itself
Create the inability to speak
Make the nerves in my body pulsate

What phenomenon threw me into such a state
Transfixed me
The blare of ancient trumpets
So off key, so dissonant to my ears
Accompanied by a slow, cadenced drum beat
Male and female members of the clergy massed in rank order
Walked behind the unadorned wooden coffin
On an unimposing, rough flatbed cart pulled by two mules
The townspeople led by their own dignitaries completed the
    entourage
That moved around the square
Towards the cathedral at the far end

I wanted to close my eyes but dared not
I wanted to clap my hands over my ears

But could not make them go there
A croak escaped my lips as I tried to communicate my terror

After a time of struggle I allowed my self to go passive
To become a spectator of myself and the event moving before me
I thought the horns would ruin my hearing
With their periodic blasts of sound
The drumbeats felt like blows upon my body
My throat strangled me, barely allowing air into my chest
My body quivered spasmodically unaffected by the warmth of the day's sun

As the procession approached the cathedral
Eight robed men came through the massive doors now opened wide
And with obvious reverence
Carried the coffin into the depths of the cathedral
The populace waited
At a signal the clergy entered
The populace waited
Another signal and all surged forward to enter

The loud, harsh sound of the horns and rhythmic thumping having ceased
I became aware of organ music from inside the cathedral
I broke free of my inability to move
Slowly walked towards the entrance
Watched as the great doors swung closed
Muffling the sound from within

For a moment I debated entering by one of the small open side
    doors
Till I knew that this death had come to me before
And I should not stay to experience it again

Fate

Part I

Recently
while enjoying the yellow, purple, red, and pastel roofs
Of northern Norway
Life took an unexpected turn
That created a pall over the considerable brightness
It caused me to reflect upon the need to banish dreariness
By creating exterior positives to counteract
The day to day bleakness of one's surroundings
It was as if a feast to the eyes
Would make it possible to successfully handle
The starkness of everyday existence
I had been told that it really worked
The suicide rate had fallen dramatically
Behavioral scientists had pronounced their bold experiment
In human engineering a rousing success

I was a visitor
Glad to not live with the almost constant cloud cover,
Frequent showers, moisture, and pouring rain
That made the days when the sun was visible
A celebration of unexpected pleasure
Men's shirts were off during the brief summer
As if bare chested the sun's rays could be stored
To ward off the moisture and chill that would return so soon
Flowers were everywhere

Part II

There were a scant three days left on our vacation
When my wife announced she felt a lump in her right breast
Her every day shower normally so uneventful
Had produced a lump not the size of a pea but a small grape
I touched and could feel it

The mammogram of a year ago had found nothing
Panicked, I suggested a flight home the next morning
But, three days later, as scheduled, we arrived home
The whirlwind caught us up
Flinging us from breast specialist to hospital
For removal of the frightening, offending lump
The blur of choices to be made was terrifying
The physicians recommended but gave no assurances
Only statistics

The internet became my encyclopedia of disease
Hours of research visiting site after site
Combing through information
Searching for studies about survival rates if you were past sixty
There were none!
The chilling data that kept appearing on the screen in front of me
Was the older you were the less effective the treatment
And that was an extrapolation from younger age studies

I desperately needed to find some brightly colored roofs

Part III

Adversity is a magnet for your true friends
They form a reservoir of positive intention
With cards, calls, and visits
Bolstering our sagging energy
Reminding us of others who have completed the ordeal
Who have been through the "lost year,"
And resumed a normal life
We are comforted by their kindness and concern
Strengthened and enabled
They are an umbrella that keeps us dry
Helping us wait for the return of the sun

Missing

Last night mean spirited and cross
I chose not to kiss you good night
It was an act of deprivation
I immediately regretted
Since it was a habit
You had learned to graciously accept
As a result I lay there ruminating silently
Not allowing myself to fall asleep
Wondering whether you wondered
What caused the kiss to be missing
Or did you not notice or miss it at all

Loss – 2

How many ways can I say, "I miss you."
I hold your hand to guide you across the busy street
We drive in the car and it is silent unless I talk to you

We cook meals together now
I take a small measure of comfort that we are doing something
Alongside each other
It is a pretense of shared preparation

Your uncertainty creeps into an activity and another and another
I thank my Scientology training
It enables me to answer the same question a dozen times
With the same soft sincere response

Holding your hand while watching a movie brings a small smile
   to your face
And a pang of pain inside me
Vos iz gevain iz gevain iz nishtu
What once was, once was, is no longer

Last Things

Let me say, "I love you"
Kiss you tenderly and then passionately
Hold your hand and stroke your fingers
Look into your eyes and view what we have shared together
Then,
I will close your eyes
Allow my tears to flow, my sobs to wrack me
Cursing God our positions were not reversed

Only then do I feel cold,
Only then can I say farewell.

Losing You

I am losing you
Like water dripping between the fingers
There is less of you I can hold.
The perplexed look on your face
Comes more often now.
I watch you turn away
Trying to hold the pain within you
So the tears that fill your eyes
Will not give me anguish

Today

Today
I
The non-believer
Asked God for help
To put an end
To the physical being
of one we both love

I willingly give up
My need to be with the remnant
That ignites my stored memories

Allow her a sleeper's goodbye

Death, Expected

The sibilant hissing
Rattles within the throat
The chest deflates
A being is about to die

The eyes grasp the remainder of the world
Then turn towards inner perceptions
A faint tremor glides and slowly subsides
A being has become a body

Lost Memories

The wet green grass sparkles in the sunlight
Reminding me of stars in the night sky
The swaying branches of the trees
Dance to a tune I can not hear

I sit reading on my porch
Occasionally pausing to watch the scene
That draws me away from the pages in front of me

Memories rush in replacing the visualization from the book
Of happier times walking along a trail in Costa Rica
Listening to howler monkeys' hoarse hoots
Communicating with each other in the swaying branches above

I enjoy the recollection for a while
Then try to push it away to be able to return to the page before me
But pain from the present intrudes

The montage of pictures on a nearby wall
Are still very real to me
A heaviness weighs on me
Knowing you can no longer access those days we spent together

Identity

Today I recognized who I once was

My view of the ground made me dizzy
My head felt too long
Saliva ran down my chin.
I forced myself into the present
By staring at a wall

When I managed to look up
There I was viewing my latest meal
Meat hanging from my teeth.
I backed away
Refusing to believe my eyes

Knowing that I have met
Me
From before
A shiver cascades through my body

Once Again

Cautiously
a new flower emerges
red from its inner heat
out of the ashes of caregiving
love of life
reappears
a slender bloom
searching for the sun
passionately new
longing to be vibrant
eager to renew and
reclaim a life with love

Bliss

I listen to the orchestra in the concert hall
Considering the length of time music has enriched my life.
My mother, now long gone, deserves credit and thanks
For exposing, encouraging, and nurturing my early interest.
As the sonic color rushes by
I smile as waves of pleasure rappel my insides.
The deluge of sound encompasses, enriches and enfolds me
Into a bliss that puts my soul at ease.

The Rainbow

I saw a dense, broad rainbow today
Arched across a portion of the sky
Vaguely anchored to the earth below
VIBGYOR flashed through my mind
As I took pains to try to identify each color
It was too far away to amuse me
With the mythic pot of gold

I marveled at its longevity
Pleased to be able to spend some time
Feeling wonder at our often beautiful world

Forsythia

The forsythia is in riot.
The concatenation crushes into the eyes
As I drive down the highway.
The occasional, misshapen, incomplete area
With spindly spires and scraggly blossoms
Creates loss, ache, and sadness
That envelop me as I view the blemish
In the tumultuous color.
Does my life parallel the forsythia?

On the Bay

My fingers are laced tightly around the wheel
Creating a slight ache in the palms
The stakes at the far side of the bay
Are still off in the distance
I glance to each side
Feel the spray's wetness on my face
Take in the blue cloudless sky
Absorb the sun's heat through my shirt
Flex my fingers to relax a cramp
Release a long held breath
There is joy in me as I move over the water

Inner Visions

Inside my head an image floats before my eyes
Of something currently not present but strongly felt
Becoming uncomfortable as my throat constricts
Muscles tensing as if I needed to run
From something in my past
Or before this past
To a time when horses and carriages
Transported me from place to place

A westerner with detailed visions
Not connected to this now

If I could evoke the past as desired
To complement the present
I'd be an encyclopedic man

Small Enjoyments

Today the sky has soft puffball clusters
Drifting aimlessly
The sun creates a tiny shadow as I stride forward

The air feels crisp
Breathing in through my nostrils
Warms it before traveling to my lungs

I am aware of my arms
Making alternating arcs
My shoulders restrain at the ends

A heaviness in my legs
Lets me know they have walked enough
Reminding me my hour is almost complete

The body heat is pleasurable
It is the sensation that pulls me back to my routine
Three times a week

Focusing on my body has cleared my mind
My life, like my routine, is full of small enjoyments

The Good Life

The sun tans my arms and creates moist heat beneath my shirt.
The day is a glorious amalgam of blue sky flecked with lazily shifting clouds.
At each step sand oozes between my toes
hindering my progress but pleasuring my contemplation if its presence.
My eyes scan the shoreline in front of me
searching for an unoccupied space I can call mine
fervently hoping no one else
will squat there before I claim it.
My blanket creates an invulnerable fortress
from which I can survey the mass of people around me.
I am able to see the waves as they race towards the shore.
There is magic watching a wall of water rise higher and higher
till the top curls foam white and crashes with a roar.
No two are alike and viewing the endless variety makes an hour disappear.
I join the brave few who challenge the waves
waiting for the exact moment to leap as high as possible and break through.
Sometimes a wave rises so high that the wall catches me,
tumbling me over and over,
carrying me towards the shallows near the beach.
My body tires from the continuous leaping.
I surrender to a wave and swim with it shoreward hurled along by its power.
On my blanket, I know life is good.

Alone

The pale blue sky
a greyish smudge that portends rain
The muffled sounds
of activity on the street
are kept from me by hurricane glass
meant to protect
My cellphone buzzes
I do not answer
needing to finish being alone
Last night I felt a pang of sorrow
that reverberated inside my body
slowly oozing into the crevices of my brain
Sleep could not come
Grudgingly
I filled the hours
with minor tasks set aside from another time
until the darkness lightened
into the pale blue sky

Autumn

Autumn is my ambivalent season
with the heat of summer slowly sliding into cool days
making the green color on the trees feel pleasurable.
The leaves starting to curl
changing through orange, yellow or brown
finally falling
create a wistfulness
that reminds me of friendships
maintained, nourished and deepened
by togetherness.
Like a season
some flower for a brief while,
others stay green for a lifetime.
A few, splendid for so long
gradually lose their color
and fade away.

Fishing

The sun sits softly overhead
Its rays surround me slowly cooking my outstretched arms
Holding the fishing rod
I am wearing sun glasses
But the intense reflected light off the water
Is too painful to focus on for more than a few seconds at a time
My eyes repeatedly are drawn back to the waves
As if I could see the fish swimming near the bottom

A finger on my line detects a tick
Creating heightened concentration
Waiting for the repeat that would galvanize me
To yank the rod upward to set the hook
But this time it does not come again
I pause for a while then reel in
To find the bait mangled
Sometimes fishing can be mostly misses

Feeling the rhythm of the waves
Standing feet braced apart
Anticipating a tick, tug or pull
In the sunshine and salt air
Satisfies the hunger to be there

The Lake

The summer sun sizzles turning me a deeper brown
The heat through my shirt has created small rivulets
I stop in the shade and let the slight breeze
Deliciously run across my body

The path I am on meanders
Well worn but now only occasionally used
The grass and weeds have started to reclaim the ground
My footprints are short term evidence of passage

Like the path I too am taking my time
Looking at the foliage
Making sure to keep my thoughts on the beauty surrounding me
Until I arrive at the lake

Togetherness

Walking along the unpaved path in the warm sunshine
There is the faintest touch of breeze
Just enough to float across our lightly clad bodies
Creating occasional momentary coolness
We talk about plans for the future
The flow of ideas roll around in the sunshine
Slowly turn until done, then languidly drift away
We have been walking for a while now
Allowing our feet to follow the path
Only marginally thinking of where we are headed
Not caring whether we ever arrive
A lull in the conversation allows heightened awareness
Of the pleasure of inhaling the air
Sensing its crispness with just a trace of dust
Our steps slow as our legs tell us they are tired
Resting in the shade of a nearby tree
We bask in the pleasure of being together

Larry

How did we become friends?
The labyrinthic exploration began with hopeful anticipation.
We chiseled away at the outer layers of our protective slate
to expose what was underneath.
Conversations warmed and deepened our interaction.
The phone became the umbilical cord that connected us.
Our relationship ripened.

Golf was a shared activity.
One day he hit the ball
turned towards me, took two steps,
his left leg crumpled and his body made a pirouette
to land on its back.
In shock I saw his half opened eyes unseeing,
heard breath raggedly escaping his throat.

I chafe at the void.
Will another mend my life?

Steve

In our family, Steve was comic relief.
He could see any situation, angled oddly.
I often marveled at his point of view
once I had finished roaring
at a piece of outrageousness.
It became a game we played.
He'd throw a curve around a corner
that would unhinge my reason and I was gone,
bereft of control, eyes wet,
red faced from the attempt to regain my composure.
I knew that once begun
the sputtering, gasping laughter
needed to exhaust itself.
Finally, I would relax and let it happen
appreciating my inability to stop,
watching myself from a distance.
He would look at me, smile, and say, "Gotcha."

Doris

She lived in Florida
in high-rise condominium
decorated in a style I'd call glitzy.
She was my aunt, my mother's sister,
living alone having buried two husbands.
Whenever I called to meet she was unfailingly enthusiastic.
We'd go to lunch or dinner
talking about plans for the future.
I enjoyed the way she doted on me.
She was caring for all her extended family.
Perhaps, subliminally,
childhood memories of playing with cousins in her house,
created a reservoir of warmth that required replenishment.
She and my mother were the generation that raised me.
Sadly, I realized that shortly I would be an elder of the family.
I allowed myself to bask in the warmth of her approval.

Election Day

The voice on the television is harsh and strident
The words are full of negative passion

I smile to myself wondering who would be taken in
By the half truths

I change the channel and for a while
A program absorbs my interest

Then another ad for the other candidate fills the screen
With too much of the same

There are programs outside of ad free PBS
I enjoy watching and I don't want to give them up

The mute button has become my constant companion
As I wait for Election Day to arrive

Touching

People slide in and out of my life,
Illuminating pieces of me
That resonate.
I glow, reflecting the meld
Of us that works.
When it doesn't
I need to slip away
From the discord that threatens
To turn ugly inside of me.

Perspective

Sometimes letting go breaks a long standing repetitive act
Like canceling a magazine subscribed to for many years
Pleasure from reading it having ebbed away

Often I hang on too long
Mostly it's just plain inertia
Change means disruption to the routine flow of things

Occasionally, I recognize that I can't physically handle a task any more
The jury rigged solutions just don't work
Reluctantly I give it up reminding myself it's ok to let go

From time to time a friendship falls apart
Leaving an ache and gap in my psyche
Wondering if I could have done something to save it
Not wanting to recognize that we have moved away from each other

Despite all this life is good

Beginning

A poem dedicated to Sarah and Jack to share some of my joy at hearing about Chad Andrew.

It is a twig with a new bud
The pulsebeat of the emerging butterfly
The turtle crawling from the sand to the sea

It is the rhizome becoming its own plant
The child with umbilical disconnected
The awesome wonder of the inception, birth

www.ingramcontent.com/pod-product-compliance
Lightning Source LLC
Chambersburg PA
CBHW072015060426
42446CB00043B/2557